"Blessed are those who believe
without seeing"

John 20:29

"This book is dedicated to my children.
Let your light shine."

Mom

Jesus isn't next to us, but His presence is always

near. Would you act the same way if He was

seen or His voice you could hear?

Jesus teaches us to love one another and kind

always be...but what if Jesus were a butterfly

that you could see?

Would you tease, ignore, and make others cry,

or help a friend in need if Jesus were a butter-

fly?

Read this book line by line, find Jesus as the

butterfly, and then decide.

It's Abby's first day at a big, new school.

She's scared she won't make friends, and her

tears start to pool. Kids laugh, point, and tease,

and Abby begins to cry.

What would you do if Jesus were a butterfly?

Would you tease her with the class? Or would

you help her tears dry? By offering a smile, if

Jesus were a butterfly.

Audrey is at the park on a bright, sunny day.

She asks the other kids if they'd like to play.

The children laugh, and their toys they don't

share. Call her names and throw sand in her hair.

As she frowns and wipes the sand from her eyes,

what would you do if Jesus were a butterfly?

Would you giggle and watch? Continue to stand

by? Or would you ask her to play if Jesus were a

butterfly?

Nolan couldn't see well. Everything was a blur. He got a new pair of glasses to see if that was the cure.

The next day at school, he could see very clear, but kids called him names and began to sneer. He wanted to hide and began to cry. What would you do if Jesus were a butterfly?

Would you laugh at him for fixing his

eyes?

Or tell him you love his new glasses if

Jesus were a butterfly.

Class ended, and Aiden was cleaning his

desk.

A kid walked by, threw his stuff to the floor,

and made a big, big mess.

Papers and books all over the floor, as the

kids stood and laughed outside the door.

You see it all happen, feel bad, and sigh.

What would you do if Jesus were a butter-

fly?

Would you pretend it didn't happen

and keep walking by? Or help Aiden

pick up if Jesus were a butterfly.

There's a birthday in class, and the child brings

treats. Charlotte's snack is bumped and falls

down by her feet.

As Charlotte began to reach for her snack, anoth-

er student grabbed it and would not give it back.

You could tell she was sad and didn't understand

why. What would you do if Jesus were a butter-

fly?

Would you pretend it never happened and

watch Charlotte cry? Or offer to share your

snack if Jesus were a butterfly.

I hope you'll act with kindness and love as you

realize now He sees you from above.

Be the change in this world and burn bright for

all to see. And never forget, Christ is within

you, and He's within me.